PARKERSBURG & WOOD COUNTY
PUBLIC LIBRARY
3100 Emerson Avenue   Parkersburg, WV 26104
http://parkersburg.lib.wv.us

EMERSON AVE. / MAIN	(304) 420-4587
SOUTH	(304) 428-7041
WAVERLY	(304) 464-5668
WILLIAMSTOWN	(304) 375-6052

COUNTRY PROFILES

AFGHANISTAN

BY AMY RECHNER

BELLWETHER MEDIA • MINNEAPOLIS, MN

Blastoff! Discovery launches
a new mission: reading to learn.
Filled with facts and features, each
book offers you an exciting new
world to explore!

This edition first published in 2019 by Bellwether Media, Inc.

No part of this publication may be reproduced in whole or in part
without written permission of the publisher.
For information regarding permission, write to Bellwether Media, Inc.,
Attention: Permissions Department,
6012 Blue Circle Drive, Minnetonka, MN 55343.

Library of Congress Cataloging-in-Publication Data

Names: Rechner, Amy, author.
Title: Afghanistan / by Amy Rechner.
Description: Minneapolis, MN : Bellwether Media, Inc., 2019. |
    Series: Blastoff! Discovery: Country Profiles | Includes
    bibliographical references and index. | Audience: Grades 3-8. |
    Audience: Ages 7-13.
Identifiers: LCCN 2018000615 (print) | LCCN 2018004378 (ebook)
    ISBN 9781626178397 (hardcover : alk. paper) |
    ISBN 9781681035802 (ebook)
Subjects: LCSH: Afghanistan–Juvenile literature. | Afghanistan–Social
    life and customs–Juvenile literature.
Classification: LCC DS351.5 (ebook) | LCC DS351.5 .R43 2019
    (print) | DDC 958.1–dc23
LC record available at https://lccn.loc.gov/2018000615

Editor: Rebecca Sabelko   Designer: Brittany McIntosh

Printed in the United States of America, North Mankato, MN.

TABLE OF CONTENTS

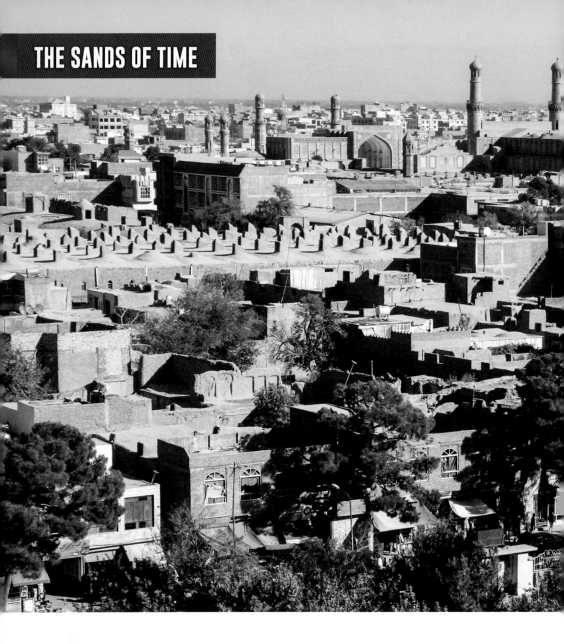

The sun rises over the city of Herat. Ancient, sand-colored buildings fill the Old City while bright, modern canopies shade shopping stalls. Soon people fill the streets, searching the **bazaar** for bargains.

OTHER TOP SITES

BLUE MOSQUE

GARDENS OF BABUR

MINARET OF JAM

MUSEUM OF ISLAMIC ART

As the sun's rays warm the day, visitors marvel at the beauty of the *Masjid Jami*, the Friday Mosque. Its tile **mosaics** are over 800 years old. Nearby is the Citadel, a fortress that was first built by Alexander the Great. Years of wars and rebuilding have left their mark. From the top, visitors see Herat spread out below. Ancient architecture meets modern-day life in Afghanistan!

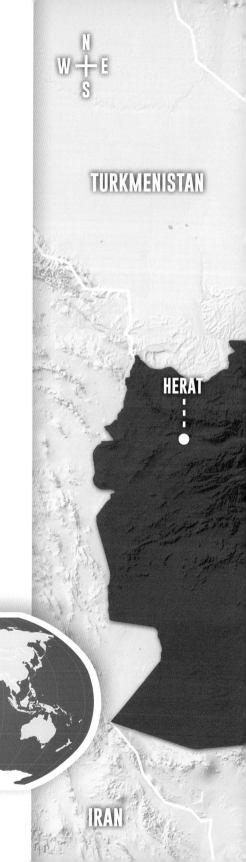

LOCATION

Afghanistan is located in south-central Asia. Slightly smaller than the state of Texas, it covers 251,827 square miles (652,230 square kilometers) of landlocked **terrain**. Iran is to the west, and Pakistan wraps around the south and east. China makes up 57 miles (91 kilometers) of its eastern border, too. Turkmenistan, Uzbekistan, and Tajikistan line the northern border.

The nearest large body of water is the Arabian Sea. It is about 300 miles (483 kilometers) south. The capital city of Kabul sits along the Kabul River in east-central Afghanistan, between two mountain ranges.

N
W+E
S

TURKMENISTAN

HERAT

IRAN

UZBEKISTAN

CHINA

TAJIKISTAN

MAZAR-E SHARIF

KABUL

AFGHANISTAN

KABUL RIVER

KANDAHAR

PAKISTAN

LANDSCAPE AND CLIMATE

About four-fifths of Afghanistan is covered in mountains. The Hindu Kush range begins in the northeast with the Pamir Mountains. It reaches all the way across the country to the southwest. Snow from mountain peaks melts to feed the rivers in the **basins** below. The

= HINDU KUSH RANGE   = REGISTAN DESERT

mountains flatten into broad **plains** in the south and west. The southern corners are desert, including the sandy Registan Desert.

HINDU KUSH RANGE
BAND-E AMIR NATIONAL PARK

PANJSHIR VALLEY

KABUL
Average seasonal highs and lows

JANUARY
HIGH: 43 °F (6 °C)
LOW: 23 °F (-5 °C)

APRIL
HIGH: 75 °F (24 °C)
LOW: 61 °F (16 °C)

JULY
HIGH: 93 °F (34 °C)
LOW: 81 °F (27 °C)

OCTOBER
HIGH: 77 °F (25 °C)
LOW: 59 °F (15 °C)

°F = degrees Fahrenheit
°C = degrees Celsius

Afghanistan has cold winters and dry, hot summers. Winters can bring snow to the Hindu Kush range or rain to the mountains along the Pakistan border. The desert area in the southwest remains dry.

9

Exciting animals fill the wild country of Afghanistan. Rare snow leopards and markhor scale the mountains. Golden jackals and Indian gray mongooses roam the **scrubland**. Long-legged urial sheep and ibex graze on grass in the northern plains. Small mammals like hedgehogs, mouse hares, and shrews flee their hunters. **Venomous** snakes, such as Persian horned vipers, hide among rocks.

Predatory birds like saker falcons swoop down from mountaintops to catch mice. Great white pelicans and flamingos linger along rivers in the Hindu Kush range, looking for fish.

MARKHOR

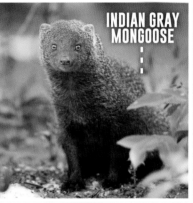

INDIAN GRAY MONGOOSE

ASIATIC BLACK BEAR

SAKER FALCON

DISAPPEARING ANIMALS

Afghanistan's Asiatic black bear, goitered gazelle, and Marco Polo sheep are hard to find these days. Years of unlimited hunting have made many animal species scarce.

SNOW LEOPARD

SNOW LEOPARD

Life Span: 10-12 years
Red List Status: vulnerable

snow leopard range = ⬛

LEAST CONCERN	NEAR THREATENED	VULNERABLE	ENDANGERED	CRITICALLY ENDANGERED	EXTINCT IN THE WILD	EXTINCT

About 34 million people live in Afghanistan. The Afghan people are a mix of many different **ethnic** groups. The largest group is called Pashtun. Others are Tajik, Uzbek, and Hazara. Afghanistan has two official languages. The most common, Dari, is a Persian **dialect**. The other is Pashto.

Islam is Afghanistan's national religion. People who follow Islam are called Muslims. Long ago Muslims split into two branches, Shi'a and Sunni. Shi'ites follow living **descendants** of Mohammed. Sunnis base their faith on Mohammed's teachings. Most Afghan Muslims are Sunni.

FAMOUS FACE

Name: **Fahim Fazli**
Birthday: **May 30, 1966**
Hometown: **Kabul, Afghanistan**
Famous for: **An actor in *Iron Man* and many other films, he also worked with the U.S. Marines as an interpreter in Afgahnistan from 2009-2010**

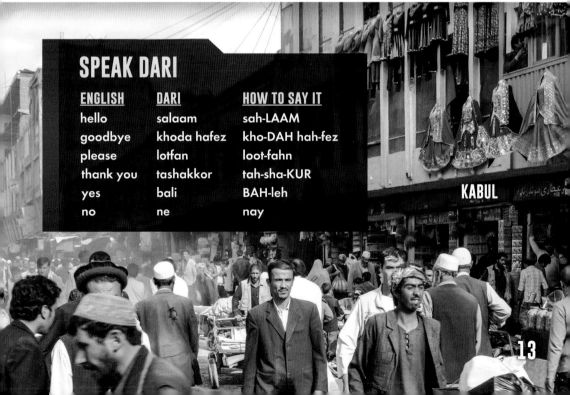

SPEAK DARI

ENGLISH	DARI	HOW TO SAY IT
hello	salaam	sah-LAAM
goodbye	khoda hafez	kho-DAH hah-fez
please	lotfan	loot-fahn
thank you	tashakkor	tah-sha-KUR
yes	bali	BAH-leh
no	ne	nay

KABUL

COMMUNITIES

An Afghan's community begins with the family. Young and old live together in large groups called tribes. Some tribes live in **rural** farm communities. **Nomadic** tribes herd animals. They live in tents and travel with all their belongings. In villages and cities, houses are simple and shared by the whole family as well. Businesses are often a part of the home.

NOMADIC TRIBE

Years of war have left Afghanistan roads in rough shape. Communities are working to rebuild their homeland. Cars are driven mostly in larger cities like Kandahar and Kabul. Public transportation is limited, but many people use bicycles to get around.

Afghanistan is a country of clans and tribes who share
Muslim beliefs and customs. One custom they all share is
hospitality. Muslims are quick to welcome people into their
homes. The typical Muslim greeting is "Peace be upon you."
Sometimes Afghans shake hands or place a hand on their
hearts in greeting.

Girls and women must always have their heads covered. Women may cover their faces, too. They cannot make eye contact with men. Ignoring such customs would dishonor the family and clan. Honor and loyalty are important.

GIRLS IN DISGUISE

Since Afghan girls have few opportunities, some parents pretend their daughters are boys. With boys' names and disguises, they go to school, run errands, and enjoy freedoms most girls do not. These girls are known as *bacha posh*.

Afghan children start primary school at age 6. Middle school begins at age 13. Some go to secondary school to prepare for a trade or university, but many do not. Wars have made schooling difficult. Children have had to leave their homes to find safety. Sometimes teachers give lessons in a tent or under a tree for **refugee** children who gather for the chance to learn.

Afghan people hold many different jobs. Some have family trades like baking, carpet weaving, or sewing. Most are farmers who grow crops, like wheat and fruit, or tend livestock. The well-educated work in office jobs.

HERDER

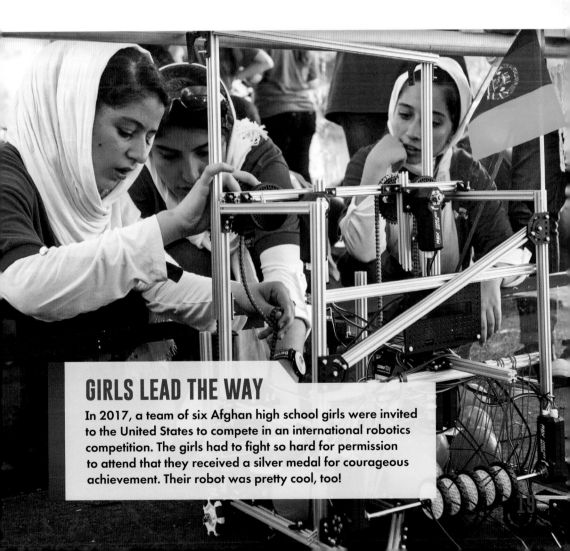

GIRLS LEAD THE WAY

In 2017, a team of six Afghan high school girls were invited to the United States to compete in an international robotics competition. The girls had to fight so hard for permission to attend that they received a silver medal for courageous achievement. Their robot was pretty cool, too!

SPORT OF HONOR

A favorite traditional sport in Afghanistan is called *buzkashi*. Many men on horseback compete to grab a goat. Once captured, the goal is to place the goat in the scoring circle. The athletes and their horses train for many years to become *chapandaz*, or champions.

Afghanistan has national teams for cricket, soccer, and basketball. Afghan **provinces** have teams that compete against each other. Fans fill the stadiums and listen on the radio. Another popular sport is kite flying. Men and boys build kites together to fly in kite fighting contests.

CRICKET

Afghan children have to grow up quickly due to the pressures of war and **poverty**. Still, they like the same games other kids do. They play soccer, hopscotch, tag, and other games. Boys like to play with slingshots. Girls sometimes have dolls made from rags or carved from wood.

KITE FLYING

JOZBAAZI

What You Need:
- sidewalk chalk
- stones

Using sidewalk chalk on a driveway or playground, draw a large court (see diagram).

| 4 |
| 3 |
| 2 |
| 1 |
| start |

How to Play:
1. To begin, the first player stands on the starting point and tries to throw their stone to level 1.

2. If the stone lands there, they must go to their stone and kick it back to the starting point standing on one leg. They can kick as many times as they need, but they cannot put their foot on the ground.

3. If they succeed, they try for level 2. If their stone does not land in the level two slot, it is the next player's turn.

4. The game continues in this way until one of the players is the first one to complete all four levels.

FOOD

TAKE OFF YOUR SHOES

Dinner guests should expect to take their shoes off. They will sit on a floor cushion, by the dastarkhan. They must be careful not to point the bottoms of their feet at the table or other guests. Everyone only eats with the right hand.

Every Afghan meal includes *naan* bread. It is a flat, oval bread that Afghans use to scoop up food. Recipes rely on Afghan farms for fruits, vegetables, and dairy products. An Afghan **tradition** is *dastarkhan*, a large spread of food laid over a cloth. The cloth is often laid on the floor.

The day begins with yogurt, sweet bread called *roht*, and eggs with herbs and vegetables. *Kabobs*, skewers of meat with vegetables, are a quick lunch. For dinner, *qabili palau* offers tender meat with raisins and carrots over rice. Dessert lovers enjoy *baklava*, squares of dough and sweetened nuts.

KABOBS

QABILI PALAU

EASY NAAN BREAD

Ingredients:
2 cups all-purpose flour
3/4 teaspoon baking soda
1 teaspoon sugar
1 teaspoon salt
1/2 cup plain yogurt
1/4 cup water
1 tablespoon oil
melted butter for brushing (optional)

Steps:
1. In a large bowl, mix the flour, baking soda, sugar, and salt.

2. In a glass, mix together yogurt, water, and oil.

3. Add yogurt mixture to the flour mixture. Knead the dough until it is soft. Cover with a damp towel. Set aside for 20-25 minutes.

4. With an adult, heat a non-stick pan over medium heat. Roll out the dough to 1/4-inch thickness. Cut it into three pieces.

5. Brush both sides of the dough lightly with water.

6. With an adult, place the dough on the heated pan. Cover with a lid. Wait for 45 seconds before flipping it over. Give it 30 seconds on the other side. Take it out of the pan. Place on a plate. Cover with foil.

7. Apply melted butter immediately and serve hot.

NOWRUZ

The Afghan New Year is on March 21, the first day of spring. It is called *Nowruz*. Afghans celebrate with feasts, formal ceremonies at **mosques**, and buzkashi matches. The holy month of Ramadan changes dates each year. Muslims **fast** from sunup to sundown. When it ends, they rejoice with a three-day festival called *Eid al-Fitr*.

Afghans decorate and fly flags for its August 19 Independence Day. *Mawlid*, the Prophet Mohammed's birthday, is honored with public prayers, poetry readings, and shared feasts. Muslim holidays account for most of Afghanistan's national celebrations. The country's love for its faith shows in its culture and traditions!

EID AL-FITR

330 BCE
Alexander the Great invades and conquers what is now Herat

1747
A Pashtun chief names himself Ahmad Shah Durrani, "pearl of pearls," and is now considered the father of Afghanistan

1219
Genghis Khan begins his conquest of the world and invades what is now Afghanistan

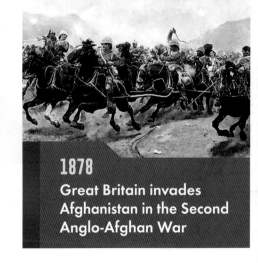

1878
Great Britain invades Afghanistan in the Second Anglo-Afghan War

1988
Afghanistan is promised the United States and the Soviet Union will not interfere in their country

1919
King Amanullah launches the Third Anglo-Afghan War, gains independence from Britain, and begins to modernize Afghanistan

2001
While stationed in Afghanistan, the terrorist group al-Qaeda commits the 9/11 attacks in the United States

1979
After decades of violent Afghan struggles for power, the Soviet Union invades Afghanistan

2017
Although the War on Terror ended in 2014, United States troops remain in Afghanistan due to an increase in Taliban activity

1996
The Taliban regime comes into power

Official Name: Islamic Republic of Afghanistan

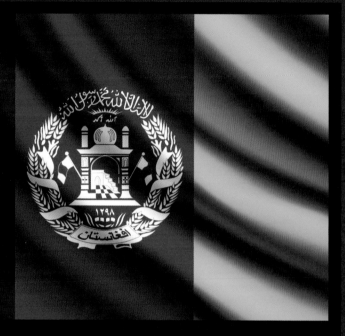

Flag of Afghanistan: Three equal vertical bands of black, red, and green. The national emblem in white is in the middle. It shows a mosque with a podium and flags on either side, circled by a border of stalks of wheat on the left and right. Above the mosque is the Muslim creed in Arabic. Below are rays of the rising sun over an Arabic expression meaning "God is great." At the bottom is a scroll that reads "Afghanistan."

Area: 251,827 square miles
(652,230 square kilometers)

Capital City: Kabul

Important Cities: Kandahar,
Herat, Mazar-e Sharif

Population:
34,124,811 (July 2017)

COUNTRYSIDE
72.4%

WHERE PEOPLE LIVE

CITY
27.6%

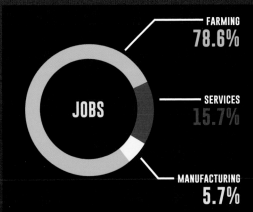

FARMING
78.6%

JOBS

SERVICES
15.7%

MANUFACTURING
5.7%

Main Exports:

wool

fruits
and nuts

carpets

National Holiday:
Independence Day (August 19)

Main Languages:
Dari and Pashto

Form of Government:
presidential Islamic republic

Title for Country Leader:
president

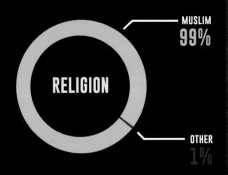

MUSLIM
99%

RELIGION

OTHER
1%

Unit of Money:
Afghani

GLOSSARY

basins—areas drained by a river

bazaar—a marketplace containing rows of small shops or stalls

descendants—people related to a person or group of people who lived at an earlier time

dialect—the local way of speaking a particular language

ethnic—related to a group of people who share customs and an identity

fast—to stop eating all foods or particular foods for a time

mosaics—images or patterns made up of small colored pieces

mosques—buildings that Muslims use for worship

nomadic—relating to people who have no fixed home but wander from place to place

plains—large areas of flat land

poverty—lack of money or possessions

provinces—areas within a country; provinces follow all the laws of the country and make some of their own laws.

refugee—a person who flees for safety

rural—related to the countryside

scrubland—dry land that has mostly low plants and few trees

terrain—the surface features of an area of land

tradition—a custom, idea, or belief handed down from one generation to the next

venomous—producing a poisonous substance called venom

TO LEARN MORE

AT THE LIBRARY

Ali, Sharifah Enayat. *Afghanistan*. New York, N.Y.: Marshall Cavendish, 2013.

Glynne, Andy. *Ali's Story: A Real-life Account of His Journey from Afghanistan*. North Mankato, Minn.: Picture Window Books, 2018.

Nardo, Don. *Understanding Afghanistan Today*. Hockessin, Del.: Mitchell Lane Publishers, 2014.

ON THE WEB

Learning more about Afghanistan is as easy as 1, 2, 3.

1. Go to www.factsurfer.com.

2. Enter "Afghanistan" into the search box.

3. Click the "Surf" button and you will see a list of related web sites.

With factsurfer.com, finding more information is just a click away.

INDEX